NATALIE ANN HOLBOROW is a Swansea-born writer of poetry and fiction. In 2015, she won both the Terry Hetherington Award and the Robin Reeves Prize, and in 2016 was named as runner-up in the Wales PEN Cymru New Voices Award. She has been commended and shortlisted for various others including the Bridport Prize and Hippocrates Prize. Natalie's work has recently appeared in *The Stinging Fly* and *New Welsh Review*. She is currently working on her first novel with the aid of a Literature Wales bursary.

For my grandparents, Julie and Steve,
my favourite double act

So many people are shut up tight inside themselves like boxes, yet they would open up, unfolding quite wonderfully, if only you were interested in them.

SYLVIA PLATH

CONTENTS

And Suddenly You Find Yourself

MOONFLOWER

When I arrived in my nightgown
he told me I must see the moonflower.
The nightdress didn't faze him,

petalled waist wrinkled with silks.
My veins in the twilight could have been
ivy thatching my bones.

I asked him: *What moon?* He lived by astronomy,
some lunar goddess batting her white eye
until even his head was a total eclipse.

He would not compare me to starlight,
nor speak of human blood.
The moonflower tight as a heart.

These stalky limbs squeeze and curl,
lifting like blades, skirts flaring
become the moon's white bride.

He wrote its name like a christening:
Ipomoea alba;
smeared chlorophyll over his shirt.

His own human skin offered to God
as though he could shed it for botany.
When it opens, will it be white?

We pale in the light of the moonflower
undressing its nerves from the earth,
this great arrival of blossoming hosts;
this ridiculous five-petalled birth.

CRAIG Y NOS

You were eight when you got the infection.
All day long, that terrible racket hacked
through the bleached sanatorium
where day after day
mucus slapped the roof of your mouth,
slid salt-green down the ridge
where your tongue was huge
and parched for weeks. Barely able
to pant the word *dŵr*.

The last time you saw Aileen Morgan,
she was all sore angles beside her bed.
Stripped from the sheets with the fever,
shuddering in her nightdress,
you remarked softly on her pretty red scarf
twisting like blood through the bars.
It was years before you got over the sight
of her, pill-shattered on her pillow,
torso shapeless and white.
The nurses let loose her cold fingers
and tucked the scarf into a box.

You were wheeled on your beds to the balcony.
In hushed voices, they said
the Welsh winds worked miracles
if they did not kill you off. One morning Hywel
raised a sick arm of chicken-flesh, tinder-bone:
please Nurse, I'm cold in a little voice.
She slapped his face barehanded.
Every morning before sunrise, she proofed herself
against tuberculosis in folds of starch and cotton,
scrubbed her hands by candlelight.
Scissors grinned from her breast-pocket.
Every day some child folded himself like a nautilus,
hacking his rags of lung into a pillow.
Your sternum became a birdcage.

BITE

I. Snow White

I laid their linen
 in dwarfish squares,
 heart breaking for these poor lambs
soft and fat, wet-eyed,
 pulling the sheets.
 No mother to kiss their fingers.
I preside over these china cups,
 butter-knives, scrubbed little spoons
 upon the tea-ringed table,
scoop cold berries from the bowl.
 Later, bored with searching
 for little boys
I float up the staircase to bed
 in a spiral of dust-motes,
 making my shadow known.
The children are on their way home now.
 I warm a small bed
 with the curve of my back,
but gasping and fished
 from a whirlpool of dreams,
 I wake to Adam's apples.

II. The Wicked Queen

It was only natural she should
 fall in love
 with the fat sweet heart
of a bad apple, what with her
 being so young
 and lustful—
silk rustling, fingers curled—
 white visions
 of her slim wrist turning the handle,

revealing herself baby-eyed
to the whistle of seven men.
The royal prince can lie back now
to his heart's content
one eye unpeeled,
sobbing and breathless—
sputtering into his hand
while she goes on unbreathing.

The red-skirted rose, her long-dead
claim to fame—
fairest in the land
so my mirror confirms,
smiling at the globes
of these queenly breasts
not even a king could resist.
See how his visions
circle like planets
where finding me here, irresistible,
old enough to have raised him
my eyes intrude
on his clammy dreams
as the morning turns,
spilling its blood-lights
and rolls through forbidden orchards.

III. The Huntsman

It was then I found myself
towering above her, throwing my axe,
a priest in bloody worship
before the trembling lamb.
I'll never forget the brilliance
of her milkwhite face,
the snowcapped curve of her shoulders
where her dress slipped

and revealed too much of her
in a cage of lean firs.
Mouth open— her horror
at seeing a man with a weapon.
Her lips wide, hair black
as the gleaming eel.
I looked away, took a deep breath
while butterflies shut
in their thousands—
yet choked by her perfume,
circled by birds,
I left her to hunt the boars.

IV. Prince Charming

I found her passed out in the forest.
Surrounded by males all sniffing their griefs
I muscled in between them—
Charming, one told me, fists curled.
I nodded *hello* to the little thug,
leaned down upon my princess
and kissed her without thinking,
having travelled too far
and much too long
alone amongst fallen apples.
Perhaps it was true love
or the nip of my incisors
that raised her then from the dead.
Yawning, her small mouth
said nothing
but riding away, girl cleaved to my side
I gave her a fairytale ending.

WONDERLAND

A smile costs nothing
                    so they say,
so I grin til she gets self-conscious;
drops her gaze to a forest floor
mottled with moss and birdshit,
          none of that
sugar and spice malarkey
where even the flowers smell like flesh.

One hundred watts of dentistry
shatter the pinetree dark, stripes vertical
                    as jail bars—
straight as sticks,
tail like a straggling vein—
          please stand and behold
the great vanishing act,
this incredible cat
                    in your candy-sucking dozens
wheezing on smoky narcotics,
my odd and neurotic
          spectator is a thousand wriggling legs
too high to do anything else but question
every fucking detail—
                              who are you?—
blaming the fumes
from those dull and knock-kneed bastards
          painting the roses red
for her Menopausal Majesty.

We're all mad here. I growl when I'm happy,
wag my tail when I'm pleased;
                              therefore I'm mad

but still—
I have stopped attending tea parties
in tasteless hats,
but grinning at everything,
everyone
and nothing at all
I will get by on a Hollywood smile
and card games,
cosmetic dentistry
and those crazy catnip nights
in Wonderland.

PENELOPE

There are several ways to deal
    with things like this. First of all
        I turned his absence into a dress
of crushed peach, wore his sailing shade
    against my hip. These sad impressions
        of the body, silk islands.

I avoided the danger of flesh-coloured
    skirts on the thigh. There are
        other things I could do:
cradle his heap of clothes
    like a baby. Drop them
        down the stairs, arrange them
into his shape and kid myself.
    Leave his scent forever on the staircase.

I could take off my shoes in the evening
    and bring his dead shirts to my nose,
        feel the weight of Ithica in my arms.
Yet in the nights, under moon-cracked skies
    I can picture him sunk in a seabed,
        have him lit like a searchlight. I think of him,
my silk skirts screwed in a stranger's fist.
    Time to move on, as they say.

I don't even notice the door click shut,
    his wrecked and shaking return.

ACHILLES

counts to ten in a plastic chair
outside the psychiatrist's door.
This is not like
being called up to army—
his name is a ribbon of silk
when she whispers it,
snaking perfumed round the door

and he snarls, scrabbles in his belt
for a sword, free hand
flapping against magazines
for his propped-up shield,
the bronze unblinking eye.
She breathes at him through her nose.
The bastards have stripped him

of everything, scrubbed him baby-clean
of glory, the crusted blood of Hector
marbled against porcelain,
swirling away Aegean.
Post-traumatic stress—
she dips the words in hot iron,
scorches it into his history

with an arrow full of ink,
earrings swinging, understanding
his outbursts, his frowning obsession
with flashback fields of wildfire,
the persistent itch in his heel
and the blood-wet Trojan sputtering,
dragged face-down through his dreams.

MEDEA

I stand in the bedroom, sweatless.
I admit to the dagger,
the rage and the kids
who looked like you; had the eye
of the cool Aegean
with Argonaut bravado
and a traitor's blood.
Our babies. I nursed them
with love and a knife
to save them from sins like you—
our lullabied young.
Like you, they were forked in the tongue.

But I was once young,
a charming girl, head over claws
in love with you—
protective, faithful
as any good angel, my Colchis light
bleaching a brother's bones.
You could say I became obsessed.
I had you possessed
but Corinth tore us apart.

Still, I can't resist revenge,
death knell shaking the house
to its dead foundations,
the children's gasping surprise;
oh, the look in your eyes
when you found them, coiled
like little white worms
or the curl of a gorgon's hair.
She may be princess
but I am a queen,
Medea—

monster maternal,
with blood in my breasts
and a glint in my milkwhite eye.
Revenge is a kick in the womb.

PORTRAIT OF THE ARTIST

A poem from the works of Dylan Thomas

They would be tittering together now
with their horrid bodies close,
their arms and legs and throats
as brown as berries.

I could hold her and kiss her, he thought—
put her straight-haired, heavy head
on my shoulder, brave enough at last
to hold her cold hand in its glove.
The lank brown horses knew it
and shook their bells, anchored among
the hulks of houses and the snow man
with the broken back.
Her chest moved up and down.

Her rough body, her bottle-legs
grew from a few words.
Laughing from the shelter of the chapel
into the darkness, this heretic
with his hand on her breast
opened his eyes with a nervous impulse,
saw the town in a daze spin by them.
There was never a young lover
who didn't love the moon, they said,
pecking each other like gulls in the air
dirty as Christ knows what.

CASTELLAMARE

What she was eating
smelled too alive,
as though it would flap
clean off the dish—

the silvered, reeking bass
widened its gluey eye
as she pronged it, tore it
with a pointy knife

crunching through salt-scaled skin
and slowly took a bite.
Her husband sat opposite
like a fat apostrophe, creamy belly

thrust out, bobbing for more.
Chewing on a hunk
of shiny lamb, he eyed her plate
until she offered. Down

his fork dived
and zipped off again,
snatching a gobbled bite,
mint sauce still smeared

like seaweed
        across his gullish lip.

LANGLAND

Gulls peeled white from mizzling cliffs,
small planets circling the sunrise.
The glitter and twist of sea-sprayed shore
silvered and rose, almost romantic
were it not for your brow cockled tight,
anxious against my cold shoulder
and feeling another year older,
you swear you'd changed overnight.
Desperate, I'd lured you into the mists
like a siren, exposed your cold bones
to the sea. But rolling your hands to stones,
sighing into your fists
you complained we'd freeze to death.
A surfer held his breath.

SEASALT

It comes beneath scudding sky, the slug of sea
singing green as glass, sucking and spraying
slate turrets, the jagged throne of Rhossili rock
where a boy squats, pink-chested
with a spade in his fist, turning pebbles.
A bumping heap of slow crabs, their wet scuttle.
Twirling a ribbon of seaweed, his grandfather bellows
in baritones, *Lavabread: salted, fried—*
da iawn, mun – coughs with a copper lung,
carrying both bucket and boy
to where a woman with loose brown skin
swings babies through the shallows,
towels their pudgy feet. She squints up, eyes
her teenage son sweating and frowning
beside the changing cubicle, half-aware
of the awkward snap of swimsuits,
the girl bundling her breasts in her arms. He knows—
seeing the cradle of rock in salty dawn
that he must spend years now hauling them,
the pearl-eyed, scaly monsters, his young skin
damp with stranger fish, his wide and roaring mind.

LONDON

For Roisin O'Connor

Your London— a fist of broken fingers
scrapes the concrete sky, half-moon blinking
down the filthy Thames;
cold-blooded, the siren's tail
seducing the loveless and raging drunk
straight from slack-jawed Highgate
into her cindered veins.

The roaring rails, grinning dogs
on their howling chains, heckle-raising
crowds swallow saltwhite fish
on a Camden stall,
side-stepping marketplace stables
where an iron horse kicks— the roaring slave
flogged to death
to the tune of cash registers, rainbow silks,
old men wheezing over pipes
to gawp at such brazen antiques
and dust-jackets older than childhood.
My saltwater hair crunches dry.

We crawl the green crown
of Primrose Hill, rolled wide by the fog
of a hundred years back, gaslight blues
where a poet's house weeps in the street.
They bring themselves, tiny,
scribbling to London
where not understanding the language of speed,
I roll in my bed like the shore.

STRANGERS

In the old house we could have been
soulmates not sisters. We chained ourselves in daisies,
your face a little flower-head turning
to find mine. My head could have been a whole summer.

On cold winter mornings we roosted like hens
in the same bunk, sharing blankets.
Today we won't share the same room.
Puberty empowered you. Your breasts

bobbed like apples under your school shirt;
bra-straps tightened, skirts hemmed up
little by little until your bare legs stretched for miles.
Once, I showed you long words in books

and your sticky small face was enchanted. Now when I read
you scoff on your lipstick, smirk through a cigarette.
Pretend we are passing strangers.
Sometimes I think of you falling into mirrors,

your hair a new shade every week.
Draping yourself around dangerous boys and stretching
your nude legs in cars. I question water and blood,
conjure the monkey-faced toddler hung across Daddy's shoulder,

stretching her fat hand towards me, making sounds
like a fierce plane. But even then you grasped for trouble,
squeezing the cat, sliding out of windows, tugging my hair
on the pillow. You hugged me hard in the grass.

I passed your new house this morning
and thought I might say hello.
You caught my sad eye across pavements.
Looked back down at your shoe.

CAWL

It was the smell of my childhood: hot stew,
warm heap of floured rolls
you cut for me, buttered
    then closed in my fist. I complained
my mouth was burning,
pressed my tongue to the soft blister
left by potato and juice. You took the spoon
from me, cooled a cube of swede with your breath.
I took a trusting bite.
Older now, and hairless, you tear cheap bread
in your hand, sigh over your spoon
    and pretend to eat. I spin a thin ribbon of leek.
Nothing in common between us now
but this bowl of chewy lamb, our unpalatable small talk.

SMOKE SIGNALS

We grew apart in inches, not miles.
The house hummed, an empty theatre,
our mother pushing the vacuum
between our silence. Hacking
clots of broken words, your lungs
drained themselves into your pillows,
fists thumping softly
until you sucked in again, stained your breath
from a chilly window. *Where are you—*
I knuckled the question into the wall
which dragged on between us, searched
with my palms for your warmth.
A blank inch pulled you away, and I listened
to those hisses, those furious sobs,
heard the weight of them
bending your spine. The vacuum
tumbled to a stop. You stopped hissing,
opened your window, blew quiet smoke
across mine.

TOWELS

The towels give you away. They surface like fish
across bedsheets, bath mats, the space you claim—
belly piercing clinking against the sink
in front of the hairsprayed mirror. Sometimes I hear them
beside baskets, heavy as mud, their damp thud
at the foot of your bed. Grinding each high heel
into the fibre, fake tan smudging your feet,
your shadow unravels from bath towels,
tugged from a sour heap. Stunned to see
I have some of you left, I heap them into my arms,
mine them from mildewed corners. Cuddle their stale folds.

CLEARING OUT THE SINGLE ROOM

I found a thing or ten of yours.
My sister with a stranger's face,
I scrabbled for any piece of you
I could save from the rubble
of your life. Pieced the lost months together
beneath that perilous chandelier
you'd chosen, plastic and shocking pink.
The light shattered into a thousand sequins.

Down on my hands and knees,
I snuffled you out like a pig.
Mascara stained the carpet
as though someone had tripped
in a pair of dirty stilettos,
charring the sticky fibres
of the rug you blazed upon
night after night,
cheap body sprays pressed
to a sickly splutter
to cover your late cigarettes.
Ashes still stuck in a musty fur
at the bottom of every handbag.

It's like one minute you were gone
and then out of nowhere
there you were again,
an oversized child
screaming out of the sock drawer,
the washbasket, howling
at the top of your lungs
from the fug of a dead slipper.
A fake eyelash clings to my finger
and says to me, *look, look*—
and I see you
clambering out of the boxes,
little girl lost in a dress.

POSTCARD

I write her a postcard to tell her
how I am. Not a real postcard—
the back of a coffee-ringed photo
of the pair of us in the same lemon dresses,
pecking ice cream cones on the wall
in the wild chill of Tenby.

In the mornings the bullish sun
heaves through everything, shatters
the greasy mirror, sours the laundry
with daylight I do not ask for.
A bottle of stolen make-up
left dribbling on the sink.

A towel sags on the doorframe
and I suck my pen trying to think.
Here, the windows have been locked
since she swung them out,
chain-smoking into the breeze.
A remembered ribbon of chemical blues.
I write my first sentence,
I'm doing fine
and do not mention
the housefly buzzing, hysterical,
butting its skull to get out.

SUNDAY

In a winter kitchen, stiff
and girlish, slurping steamy clots
of hot gravy, I am waiting

for you, rain-blistered,
with a newspaper tucked in your armpit,
carton of milk in your fist.
Pennies dazzling your pockets. You,

calm. An engine killed on the road.
Perhaps I am waiting
for the beery breeze of your shirt
zigzagged in all the wrong buttonholes,

the wonky smile
which makes you a stranger
in the wet window.
The dog circles you like a moon.

CABLES

After my father left, I found
him five days later, working
with cables as if nothing had changed.
Squeezing pliers, a handful of tape
to stick them all together
in strips of summer blue.
I crouched there, hunched like a ragdoll
forgotten, spying and ashamed.
As he tugged and grasped
I watched him twine the slim asps
round his knuckles, clip colours, and I saw
for one moment only, his frown
through the weepy steam of his tea
a split-second sparkle, *I'm sorry.*

HOME

The last time I felt it, my body small
and hard as a gulls' egg
washed and brown by the bay, my sister
moved wide and spinning
through a whirlwind of sopping foam—
          dropped
                    down
          on hilltops.

I am bigger now,
confused, but still following
          her little feet
whispering through daffodils.
We crawl to the edge of the earth.

I do it now—
          push my awkward body
stupidly beneath picnic benches,
through sticky firs,
trek circles around war monuments,
          knees shunting through the grass.

I drop,
          drag every breath.
Hot and ashamed, the green rasp
against my palms
as I call back,
call and call
beneath a cry of creamy gulls—

a woman now, silky-thighed
with poppies inked on her ankles,
a woman
          searching for home.

BLACK DOG

"I am in that temper that if I were under water I would scarcely kick to come to the top."

JOHN KEATS

He woke me just this morning, nose pushed
to my sleepy cheek, breath shuttling
down my cool neck: my faithful black dog.
His tail clubbed me all shades of violet.
The sun disc-sawed me in half.

He follows me to the kitchen.
Here he comes, his canine shape
gleaming like polished jet. I stoop
over my coffee, hiss at him to go.
My mouth lands on his drooping ear
but the stupid dog is deaf;
his dumb tongue a dripping slab
searching my hand like a rodent.
When milk won't do, he loves the sting of salt.
He nuzzles the lid of my eye.

Wherever I go, he follows.
At office desks, restaurant booths,
hunched in the seat of a taxi,
my faithful dog sniffs out my bones.
When lovers come, he turns possessive.
I wriggle free from their fingers,
stop them kissing the sides of my jaw.
They leave when I talk to the papered wall.
I grieve when their footsteps have died.

I go to bed at odd hours
to watch the small pulse of blue time.
When sleep stands me up for the zero moon,
the dog strikes me down with his paw.

PHARMACY

She meets my eye and yawns,
hair bright as a plate of lemons

and tells me to take a seat
with the others, pill-faced

and starving—
soothed by beady capsules

that heal us quicker than Christ.
A handful to settle her nervous tic

where her husband, wrapped at home
in a makeshift deathbed

gorges on daytime TV—
anaesthetised, sighing out

big words, *serotonin*—
his grey and mushroomed brain.

This man-sized baby, rattling bottles,
wailing for water and pills.

Is this for yourself, madam?
Rain blisters and pops on the door.

A name is tossed out like a sandwich-crust
as I wait my turn, eye the cool blink

of dark bottles, elixirs,
bored ladies in white

diamond-mining the shelves
for the perfect cure

to rock me to sleep at long blue last
in the blank of my outstretched hand.

AFTER SUMMER

The burnt breeze has come
too early,
skewing in through the wide
shock of a patio door.
I sit on the stained carpet
and make myself breathe
the canned-heat shimmer
of nobody's yard
trembling up
from a haze of brambles and bonfires,
brown weeds
and tangles of parsley-green
keeping their wet distance.
Blank wigs of smoke
unravelling
to ribbons
slyly fugging
these rooms of citrus
and gin—
exhaling around me,
mimicking breath.

BURNT TOAST

The kitchen reeks of stale arguments
and bacon. She glances up, horrified,
rasher dangling like a sock
between her fingers
as I show up, half-chewed
in my father's oversize fleece.
Between us, all you can hear
is the sound of a butter-knife scraping.
Oiled fingers. Burnt toast. She offers,
eggs me on to eat. I say, calmly,
no thank you, it's burnt
as she stands, arms crossed, watching me
shred cucumber into fifty wet pieces,
slide tomatoes around my plate,
not knowing

how I have trembled all night
from this stack of bones, squeezed
the soft bits like clay.
There, I say, and glare at her,
waving my bare fork as evidence.
Swallow a cold frill of lettuce.

MIRROR

Her eyes remind me of staring down
    into the dregs of a cola cup
left in a warm sink,
    that same unremarkable shade
of wet rust on a bicycle frame.

If I had loved her, I could have told her
    that her eyes looked remarkable
in the wasting light, rays
    quietly ageing our shadows.
Perhaps I could have described to her
    the woody shade of almonds
scattered in somebody's fist.
    The burning cap of a field mushroom.

I stare and stare back at those eyes
    until the steam hides her away,
and all I can see is a formless blur
    shunting about the bathroom,
grappling for towels.

THE FEMALE NUDE

I have done it. I have done it in this room
in broad daylight: unravelled myself to the human shape,
shown them the flush of my cheek. I shoulder away
my silk scarf, seize a whole breast in my hand.
The lamp gawps. Under the glass eye
my boot tips, a leather confession.

This is the shape of the female nude,
my bald toes ten revelations.
I have scattered my string of shy pearls.
They vanish in heaps of blue silk, gold rings,
the virginal cotton blouse.
Shutters whir and snap, the black eyelid,
capturing my ankles, soft arms,
the teetering sway of my hips.
Skin cells, not pixels. Resolutions of flesh.
This is the body of woman.

DELTA OF VENUS

He stretched himself alongside her to smoke a cigarette
with all the ceremony of an opium dreamer.
He felt for her heart where her breast clung to his hand.

He wrung her nose, struck her on the cheeks
and bent her fingers. He held her pulses hard,
a body so smooth no bones ever showed,
much more like fire than light. He watched her with fascination.

The sun dried her. His hands touched her rich hair
and braided it, one strand losing itself among the bedclothes
where he found it later, shining, electric.
Venus, fastened in the arms of Adonis, beat his embracements

with her heels. He held her feet in his hands, locked her
with such a force that her bones cracked. She laughed in her chains
and said, *You're suffocating me,* then fell back, became herself—
sea and sand and moisture in a Chicago apartment.

Graze on my lips, she commanded, *and if those hills be dry stray lower.*
He got impatient with the skirt. He would not put out the light,
his mouth on her throat, kissing the words he could not utter,
each several limb doubled. Twined about her thigh to make her

stay. Now it's dark and he's on his knees in the living-room
like a pilgrim before his television, arrested by the sight of a man
trying to pull a nude body from the sea. He cannot take a shower
without remembering the feel of her wet skin, plucking a clean
towel. Remembers Venus emerging out of the sea.

COUP DE FOUDRE

I suppose this is being adults. Slim candles.
    Oysters, coughed out like clots of phlegm
from filthy shells. Perhaps you think you'll
seduce me with the float of your brow,
the thin smile above your collar starch
you've practiced in the mirror. Tip champagne
down your throat and pretend to like it.
Swallow a belch. You make some vague comment
about French wine, *Provence*, *Bordeaux*
you might have once seen on a classroom map
or your mother's trolley, her frizzed hair
drifting through the aisles like cumulus.

    The menu purrs, *du, de la*, like a fly
stuck fast in the laminate, swimming on a plate
of *foie gras, bouillabaisse.* Look at you,
a connoisseur at last, sticky as boiled ham
in your high street shirt. I swallow a mouthful
and swill it around my tongue. You blush.
I do not pretend to taste *pamplemousse*,
crushing in the winepress grapes of Champagne,
the sputtering *Veuve-Clicquot*.

THE PARTY

I drew to part them: in the instant came
a madness most discreet—
he sprang over the cocktail table
and grabbed her by the throat.
The moon had risen higher
and floating in the sound
was a triangle of silver scales
trembling a little to the stiff, tinny drop
of the banjoes on the lawn.

She was laughing. *You even make love like a kid.*
Romeo, scaring the ladies like a crow-keeper,
punched her in the stomach.
I drew to part them: in the instant came
the fiery Tybalt, with his sword prepared,
a pair of stage twins, who turned out
to be girls in yellow and Clemenza
had stepped back hastily to avoid being hit
with fragments of skull, bone and blood.

The people in the street cry *Romeo—*
Rosaline, in trembling opal
seized a cocktail out of the air
and moving her hands like Frisco
danced out alone on the canvas platform.
Let's get out, whispered Jordan, after a somehow
wasteful and inappropriate half-hour.
This is much too polite for me.
Johnny sat on the floor with his head in his hands.
Here at the wedding feast, some young matrons,
wide-hipped, wide-mouthed
with all the admired beauties of Verona
slunk off in the direction of the cocktail table.

There lies that Tybalt—
and Juliet, bleeding, warm
in her pink formal gown, a tiara of flowers
in her glossy hair.
She turned to Miss Baker for confirmation.
An absolute rose?
I know your wife, continued Gatsby, almost aggressively
as Romeo thrust his maids to the wall,
and Capulet stepped out of the shadows,
threw a silken cord around his neck.
Sonny leaned back in the swivel chair
then asked in Italian, *Have they shot him?*

Then I heard footsteps on the stairs
and in a moment
the thickish figure of a woman
blocked out the light from the office door.
Probably it was some final guest who had been away
at the ends of the earth
and didn't know the party was over.

FIRST KISS

He kissed me quite by surprise.
I could feel his mean little smile
as he turned from the passenger window,
swung his face to mine,
a half-moon hooked in his hair.
The streetlights fluttered.
His tongue shot out like an arrow
and everywhere, I felt him—
fingers climbing
this staircase of rib, these breasts
round as pearls. His hands, I remember,
were clammy, having trapped them
beneath my skirted thighs
for the whole small-talking journey
and outside the window,
a childhood shape
ran laughing away to the moon.

Turning slyly, his palm coasted
my hip, drilled his thumbs at the bone.
Kissing for the first time,
the stars were nothing more
than a flicker we just got used to.

GHOSTS

A.

My twenty-year old lover on a keyring
had a smile like a shattered plate.
I liked his crooked ways; his broken lips
were a sugar bowl glued back together.
I feel his mouth out of photographs
    blowing my perfumed neck,
sucking my petalled ear.
I pressed to his light like a flower,
    chased his sly rays,
    his dirty, vanishing glow.

J.

You were awkward in that smoky night
despite your Northern swagger,
sleek-haired charm and trimmed moustache
floating a nervous millimetre
above your lip. Still, it didn't
    move you from boy to man
when I touched you
with the light on
    and you hid yourself,
    shy as a rabbit.

L.

Every room felt like a crime scene.
Our outlined shapes in chalk on the bed
from those nights when we half-bothered
to arrange ourselves like lovers.
Some nights the crease of your hip was unbearable,
the warm nut of your nipple tedious.
Some nights we cheated with sleep.
    The shape of you more stubborn,
    more real than teeth.

FROM ASIA

You send me a picture from Asia.
Shuddering and towelled in a hotel room,
the bath fills softly behind
as you pause for breath in the mirror,
slide your glasses away.
Take a photograph in the glass.

Not a duty-free smoke but a biro
propped in your tired hand,
words and wine and water,
rippled folds
are a second skin.
Your words go on for hours.

Drifting off, I may think of you,
inkstained—
coiled in a Chinese dream
in a borrowed bed,
seven hours ahead
as I wake the next morning to cherry-skies
and find it at my bedside, a poem—
a page full of you.

In return, I could answer in stanzas:
slip this paper across time-zones.
Neon scorched on your glasses
you frown over coffee and street-maps
and waving, ask for directions.
Like a pearl or a family secret,
hiraeth rolls from your tongue.

HALVES

We move from room to room in halves—
                    like burglars, approach doors and shadows
with caution, afraid of eyes blown open in anger,
                              the uncharted guest room
where I find you coiled in white
sheets, making a point of your distance.

And so everything becomes about distance,
                    bones pinned together in awkward halves
but never quite touching. We are stiff-white
                    and irreparable. Lying loose-haired in the shadows
of this fractured double room,
our silence breaks its anger

both knowing it is this anger
          that has your back rising away. You keep your distance
packing for work, making enough room
          for lateness. Already forgotten, dust-filmed halves
of human hearts beat in the bedside shadows,
two red shocks against wallpaper-white

and plonked between blister packets: those white
          measured doses, cures for anger,
smiles inked on prescription. Not your fault when the shadows
          arrive, eyes blinking into the distance.
Remember patients slumped in rows, leaning on other halves,
the nurse sighing your name through the waiting-room.

Only now there is no room
          for excuses like burning both ends. Your face could be white
with sickness, you could tell me how your life halves
          itself minute by minute, but where once I was patient,
I feel only anger,
finding our hotness infectious. Eight-thirty, and in the distance
hills toss their lonely shadows

and you drive to work, those same shadows
bruising your eyes, crossing the room
with an air of distance
that demands that no one asks questions. Cheap tie,
off-white shirt stuffed in, you swallow a mug of hot anger
and return all good mornings in halves.

All the while you pretend to work, this room of white
splits from the distance. I pack your half in a box
marked 'anger',
dump it outside on the drive. Deep in the shadows
of bloated clouds, something trembles and halves.

PANIC BUTTON

I see a tray sling in the air, a green plastic cloud
raining milk and peas and vegetable soup.
All through breakfast McMurphy's
talking and laughing a mile a minute,
teaching Joan to play the bottom half
of *Chopsticks* while he plays the top
and Lenny trying to bite
Doreen's hip through her skirt.
Mad Jimmy just keeps playing
with the Panama in front of the mirror
and making little awesome sounds
where Hemingway sits down to arm-wrestle
Ellis nailed against the wall
in the same condition they lifted him
off the table– the same shape,
arms out, palms cupped.

The girls look awfully bored to me.
I see them on the sunroof yawning,
painting their nails, bored with
knives, forks, spoons, metal dolls—
a paper Halloween bat
hanging on a string,
a snap of Roy reaching climax
while jacking off—
standing in a line like zombies
among shiny copper wires
and tubes pulsing light.
Marco picks up an avocado.
Yeah that's what an avocado is:
frozen sun. We eat the sun and then
we walk around feeling warm,
I blurt, since Doreen has suddenly
gone dumb as a post.

I remember the way he closed one eye
and looked down across
that healing wine-coloured scar,
the table shaped like a cross—
silhouette wrists and ankles
running under the leather straps.
Marco's eyes extinguished.
You're my favourite living poet,
he said. *But you're fucking crazy.*
Hemingway took off his clothes
and laid down flat on the floor.

I left Marco on his hands and knees,
scrabbling in the darkness.
The needle hung there from his pants
like a little tail of glass and steel.
Dumpy and muscular
in her smudge-fronted uniform,
the wall-eyed nurse rolled her eyes
and ducked her mouth to laugh in her fist.
It's a full moon tonight.
I open my fingers a crack and smile
at the silver globe cupped in my palm—

smile and smile at what's left of him
oozing out of his pants and shirt.

RED LIGHT

The wet streets are black enough
that you have to mount the pavement
with agonizing precision,
flowers dangling from wire baskets,
dead scatter of leaves,
and the plants like limp chickens
thudding ungraciously to the kerb.
A begonia clings to your shoe.

Perhaps this isn't what you wanted.
Perhaps what you'd hoped
was to throw yourself out
into an ocean of clean faces
who would sail past stylishly
beneath clouds of styled hair,
for the throb of their heels
to tremble up
through tarmac, fresh rainfall,
through you. Stars buzzing
like streetlamps. White teeth.
Your trousers fray and swing.

Splutter into the moon of your fist,
heaped in the passenger seat
of a slow taxi. Scatter pound coins
on the dashboard.
Slide the rest across bars.
You crunch on peanuts and wait
for the flutter of late women.
You worship each one
her stale familiarity—
the cheap bra strap
slithering loose from spaghetti vests,
fling a wet kiss on her neck.

Now she lures you, smiling
through blank cigarette inches—
within hours, heaping your bollocks
into each moistened palm,
weighting your hands
with the swell of her natural breasts.

You wake in the shrinking bedroom
of your mid-life, eat toast
in a stained bed. This, you once believed,
was where the magic could happen.
This mangle of sheets. Pillows
flung out, exhausted.
A car horn instead of a cock-crow
wakes you again, flinging the sheets
to gaze up half-romantically
over the steering wheel of your life,
at the red eye lit like a planet,
the perpetual colour of traffic.

AND SUDDENLY YOU FIND YOURSELF

in your black-lace knickers and your
early twenties, feet cold and bald
in a house nothing like
your childhood home.
Lipstick and mould.
Your teenage years dead on the rug.
A miniature hell, this grey affair
with a fusty-smelling settee
and a bottle of something red
taking acid breaths
upon the ringed table
you used to crush out menthols.

And so it goes
you quit smoking, and sulking,
chew gum for days on the stairwell.
The mirrored room
sharpens everything but yourself.
Another shadow slips in beside you,

single as an armchair,
stuck to his front like a monkey,
his muscled pack of warmth.
Your spine unzips
and suddenly you find yourself
open and gasping, newborn-blue
and just as needy. Home trembles
and calls you back
in your mother's voice

and suddenly you find yourself
squinting at stars, finding
in your own shadow the stain
of another waving back.

His face on the face of the moon.
And suddenly you find yourself
breathing and pale, looking back
at someone not quite yourself

and something that may
or may not have been love
leaking from under your rib.

THE LOST ONE

My thighs pressed at the edge of cold faux-leather,
I crackle back, stare at the blank screen between us.
The sonographer frowns, trails icy gel
between the poles of my hips.
Friends will come, awkward and silent,
tulips nodding from their fists

long after we skid from the car park,
rain gingerly ticking the windscreen.

You jam the car in the drive. I hurl these notes
from empty arms, scatter her finite story.

JACKDAWS

In the last days of his life
he lay there all day, one eye cracked open—
watching squirrels streak the windows
like meteorites. I propped him up
as he sucked and wheezed,
phlegm smacking his throat,
slippery gold
he spat in a paper cup.
His last smoke was a Cuban
on his fiftieth birthday.
I waited for the next breath.

Crushed like a nettle, this bulk of a man
who'd fought in wars, shouldered a gun;
ducked and dropped in the trenches
looked at me with drowsy eyes,
tube wriggling up one black nostril,
slack-jawed and dribbling with drugs.
I buried a kiss on the side of his head,
felt his slow pulse on my mouth.

The breath sputtered out like a blossom.
Pulling the sheet to his chin, the nurse
being kind, touched my arm softly;
gave me a minute to gather myself
and carry my silence outside
where jackdaws tugged worms
from the hospital lawn,
unpeeling themselves from the world.

HOMECOMING

Today she feels the wet coil of her brain, synapses
frazzled to smoky violets. White volts. She twists her body
    to the window, taps the purling rain, every hair bristling

the scoop of her neck. A panic attack on the bus.
Her old wool gloves have acquired
    an entirely new shape, reminiscent of dead birds.

The bus hisses to a halt. She can smell already
a wreck of overfilled ashtrays, clothes,
    curled magazines, dirty dishes left by the bed.

Here, the moon won't go home in the morning,
swings its white eye to the pavement where a bag
    keeps rolling about, small as a smacked gull.

Her phone trembles in her fist, brings her back
    as she lifts the brass key, calls: *Mam.*

ACKNOWLEDGEMENTS

Acknowledgement is due to the editors of the following journals and magazines in which some of these poems, or earlier versions of them, first appeared: *The Stinging Fly* and *New Welsh Review.* Acknowledgement is also due to the editors and publishers of anthologies in which this work has appeared: *Cheval 6* (Alan Perry, Jonathan Edwards: Parthian), *Cheval 7* (Alan Perry, Jonathan Edwards: Parthian), *Cheval 8* (Alan Perry, Jonathan Edwards: Parthian), *Cheval 9* (Jonathan Edwards, Rose Widlake: Parthian) and *How To Exit A Burning Building* (Christina Thatcher, Rachel Trezise: Parthian).

I am grateful to Aida Birch and the Terry Hetherington Award judges for their enduring support, and to Colm O'Ciarnain, Dominic Williams and Kultivera in Sweden for the opportunity to be part of the Dylan Thomas International Literary Residency in Tranås. Thank you to Geoff Haden and Matt Hughes at the Dylan Thomas Birthplace for the Versifier role and for providing some wonderful inspiration.

I am indebted to the late Nigel Jenkins for his invaluable advice and honesty, and for believing in me when I most needed it. Special thanks to Professor John Goodby for helping me shape so much of this collection, and to the encouragement of Swansea University's talented Creative Writing department. To Alan Kellermann, thank you for your editing of this collection.

Loving thanks go to all my friends, family and colleagues, for your unconditional support and for putting up with the sulking when the words wouldn't flow. I do notice, and this book is for you.

Finally, thank you Matt Jacob. Your support makes all the difference, always.